THE AMBER ROOM

THE AMBER ROOM

The year 2003 saw the completion of work on the re-creation of the famous Amber Room justly regarded as the "eighth wonder of the world". The fact that the famous interior has been opened to the public in the Catherine Palace at Tsarskoye Selo during the celebration of the tercentenary of St Petersburg is deeply symbolic. The Amber Room, a work of art produced both by 18th-century masters and present-day restorers, who have brought it back to life, serves now as a symbol of the Catherine Palace, one of the most brilliant museums of the northern capital of Russia.

The Amber Room with its mysterious history has attracted attention of Russian society in the course of more than half a century. The investigation of documents found in German archives enabled researchers to discover new facts and to correct some mistakes associated with the creation of this monument.

**PLAN OF THE FIRST FLOOR
OF THE CATHERINE PALACE**

The Prussian King Frederick William I presented the Amber Room to Peter the Great in November 1716. In return, the King of Prussia received as gifts of the Russian Tsar a small ship built in St Petersburg, 55 grenadiers for the King's regiment of giant soldiers, a lathe and an ivory goblet he himself had produced.

At the turn of the 1700s, Frederick III, Elector of Prussia (the future King Frederick I), undertook a reconstruction of Lietzenburg (later known as Charlottenburg), the suburban palace of his consort Sophie-Charlotte. It was probably then that an idea to create a unique interior of amber panels was born. Many architects including such notable figures as Johann Arnold Nering,

The Catherine Palace from a bird's-eye-view

Anonymous Russian painter. The Russian Grenadiers. *First quarter of the 19th century*

Benoit Coffre. Portrait of Peter I. 1716

The Charlottenburg Palace. Early 18th century

Jean de Bodt, Andreas Schlüter, Christian Eltester, Johann Friedrich Eosander and Philipp Gerlach the Younger contributed to the creation of this masterpiece. In 1701, the amber carver Gottfried Wolfram started the

*Alexei Zubov.
The Summer Palace. 1716*

A. *Pesne.* Portrait of Frederick William I. *1710*

J. Harper
Portrait of Frederick William I. *1722*

production of its amber decor. By the summer of 1706 one wall and details for the other had been ready. In 1707 the master craftsmen Gottfried Turau and Ernst Schacht replaced Wolfram. But they failed to

complete their work in time because Sophie-Charlotte died and the king suspended the work. In 1709 he took a decision to decorate with amber panels the gallery of Oranienburg, one of the richest royal palaces of Prussia. The palace's inventory of 1743 mentions 32 mirrors dividing the walls and arranged in pairs; similarly to the design of the room at Tsarskoye Selo. This scheme was offered by Johann Friedrich Eosander who supervised the construction work at Oranienburg. However, the gallery at Oranienburg was not completed — Frederick I died in 1713 and after the accession of Frederick William I all expensive projects in the palace were suspended. By that time the ready amber panels were kept in the Armoury Chamber of the Royal Stables. The king ordered to use them for the decoration of a small study in the Berlin Palace. This study was the first and last place in Berlin where the panels had been kept before their sending to St Petersburg.

Packed in 18 boxes, the panels were delivered to Königsberg and then, via Memel and Riga, brought to St Petersburg in the middle of 1717

The panels were carried to the wing of the Summer Palace running along the Fontanka and probably stayed there until 1743 when Elizabeth, Peter's daughter, ascended the throne. Her official residence was the new Third Winter Palace designed by the architect Francesco Bartolomeo Rastrelli. The Empress ordered to make use of the amber panels in the decor of the Audience Room intended for official receptions. For bringing together all available amber details,

Mikhail Makhayev. The Third Winter Palace. 1750
Heinrich Buchholz. Portrait of Empress Elizabeth Petrovna. *1768*
The Amber Room in the Third Winter Palace in St Petersburg (1754–55). Version of Alexander Kedrinsky. 2000

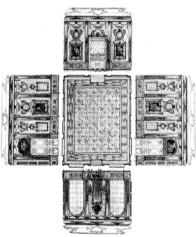

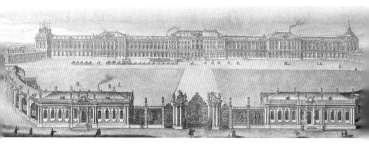

Rastrelli decided to employ mirror pilasters in carved gilt frames. Their wooden details such as window surrounds, door jambs and cornices were all carved in limewood and polished to imitate amber. During the setting of the panels three richly ornamented amber frames with mirrors were discovered. Frederick II commissioned to make the fourth, symmetrical one as a present to Elizabeth. The decoration of the room was completed in 1746.

In 1743, the construction of a new residence for Elizabeth began at Tsarskoye Selo. In 1752, the Empress invited Rastrelli to work there and he designed a magnificent palace surrounded with parks and garden pavilions for her. The Great Palace had two fine suites of rooms. The 250-metre long Golden Suite running alongside the state courtyard was particularly remarkable for

Mikhail Makhayev.
Panorama of the Great (Catherine) Palace.
Mid-18th century
The Amber Room. 1917.
Copy of a colour autochrome
View of the Catherine Palace through
the railing of the Main Gate

its luxury. Its rooms were richly decorated with gilt carving, painting and silk. Joining the architect's searches for unusual decorative materials, the Empress remembered about the Amber Study in her Third Winter Palace. In July 1755, the study was carefully dismantled, put into boxes and a special team brought the panels keeping them in their hands to Tsarskoye Selo. To arrange the amber panels in the Catherine Palace, Rastrelli designed there a special room, 96 square metres in size, but it proved t

Königsberg. Before 1944.
Photograph

The Amber Room
at the Royal Castle
in Königsberg. 1942.
Photograph from
the Pantheon magazine

Soviet soldiers
hoisting the banner
over the building of the Lyce
at Tsarskoye Selo. January 19
Photograph

The Golden Suite of the
Catherine Palace. 1944.
Photograph

be too spacious for the available details and the architect had to resort to mirror pilasters again. Besides, he covered the space between the cornice and the surface of the ceiling as well as the tier running along the lower part of the walls with painted decorations imitating amber mosaics. The painting of the upper tier was complemented with carved and gilt compositions and luxurious sculptural overdoor ornaments. According

The Great Hall of the Catherine Palace. 1944.
Photograph
The Catherine Palace. The Great Hall

to the project, the decor was to be completed by two elegant amber corner tables, each supported by a curved foot.

In the 1750s the stone-cutter Louis Siries made in Florence several mosaics after sketches by Giuseppe Zocchi. The Florentine mosaics depicted allegories of the five senses: sight, taste, hearing, touch and smell. The mosaics were placed in amber frames instead of paintings. In 1758, the Prussian craftsman Friedrich Roggenbach was invited for carrying out a minor restoration work. He became the

curator of the Amber Room and later headed the production of amber articles in the Amber Workshop at Tsarskoye Selo. In 1765, the collection of amber pieces began to take shape. In the 19th century sixty articles were put on display in showcases installed at the pier of the Amber Room.

Several German and Russian master craftsmen worked for four years together with Roggenbach

The Picture Hall
The Amber Room.
Western wall
The Crimson Pilaster Room

during the last phase of the interior decoration with amber. About 450 kilograms of amber went into the decoration of the amber pedestals supporting mirror pilasters adorned with inlaid patterns. The decorators also adapted for their work the previously not employed details delivered from Berlin, such as amber masks with carved garlands of fruit. In 1771, the overdoor decoration, brought unfinished from Berlin, was completed. The parquet floor for the room was produced later to a design by the architect Vasily Neyelov. Since Rastrelli left the ceilings

Panorama of the Amber Room
after its re-creation

in the Amber Room white, Andrei Stakenschneider later selected a suitable ceiling painting for it in the Hermitage — *Wisdom Protecting Youth from Temptations of Love* by Francesco Fontebasso.

The decor of the Amber Room demanded its permanent keep-up in due state. After drying amber was subject to destruction and crushing into small pieces, but restoration of the interior did not take place until the end of the eighteenth century. During the next, nineteenth century the amber decor was repeatedly renovated. In April 1913, Nicholas II

The decor of the upper part of an amber panel
The Amber Room →

Cornice with carved decor
Medallion of the Large Frame.
Panel of the northern wall.
Decorative top of the Large Frame.
Panel of the northern wall.
The northern wall. Detail

ordered again to carry out a regular repair in the Amber Room, but the outbreak of the First World War prevented restorers from fulfilling this project.

In 1917, after the February Revolution, the Artistic and Historical Commission headed by Georgy Lukomsky, an eminent historian of art, began to work at Tsarskoye Selo. The commission undertook a detailed photographic recording of the interiors and most valuable objects in the palaces of Tsarskoy

Selo. It also organized the making of an autochrome of the Amber Room on glass and nowadays this invaluable work is the only representation of the room in colour. In 1933–35 the architect I. Krestovsky undertook the first large-scale restoration of the room in the post-revolutionary period. The room, however, turned out to be in a poor state again as early as 1940. It demanded a restoration in stationary conditions that was planned for 1941. But the outbreak of the war in 1941 did not allow to realize the project, although the assembling and systematization of the fallen-off fragments of the background mosaics and mouldings carried away to the hinterland, gave a material of great value for the re-creation of the Amber Room in the post-war years. The evacuation of the museum values from the

Details of panels of the lower tier
Lower panel with the coat-of-arms of Frederick the Great

suburban palaces of Leningrad began immediately after Germany had declared war against the Soviet Union. The museum's members of the staff, mostly women, packed the exhibits into wooden boxes in the Church Anteroom of the Catherine Palace, loaded them and dispatched the priceless collections to the rear (to Gorky, Novosibirsk and Sarapul). The first to be saved were paintings and objects of decorative arts. The last echelon with the collections that succeeded to leave the city departed on 23 August 1941. The objects that the staff failed to send to the rear were carefully packed and taken to the basements of palaces. From that time until 15 September the museum collections were moved from Tsarskoye Selo only to Leningrad where they were preserved in the basements of St Isaac's Cathedral. The Amber Room was also

*Lower panel with the monogram
of Frederick the Great*

intended for evacuation. The amber mosaics were pasted over with a thin layer of cigarette paper, but a test removal of one of the panels demonstrated that the amber inlays crumbled in large areas. So a decision was taken to make the conservation of the Amber Room on the spot. For this purpose the panels were additionally pasted over with gaze and overlaid with sheet wadding. The windows of the room were sheathed with two layers of planks and the space between them was filled with sand.

Details of the carved wooden decor of the frieze. The southern wall

The Nazis seized Pushkin on 17 September 1941 and stayed there till 24 January 1944. Almost simultaneously with the advanced detachments of the German troops representatives of the Kunstkomission came to the town. One of the leaders of the Nazi Party mentioned about the Amber Room in his letter to Erich Koch, the last Gauleiter of Prussia: "Perishing in the fire of the war are many cultural and historical values of world significance. It is probable that this lot may befall to the great works

Overdoor decoration.
The northern wall

...y outstanding masters and to the Am-
...er Room, the national pride of Ger-
...any, now at the Catherine Palace in
...e town of Pushkin (Tsarskoye Selo).
... is necessary to take all measures
...r returning this masterpiece to the
...therland, and since it is produced
... Prussian amber, it should be taken
... Eastern Prussia, to Königsberg."

The panels were dismantled within
... hours, carefully packed and dispatch-
... to Königsberg, where they arrived

*Corner table and candelabrum clock in the form
of tree featuring a pastoral scene (1750, Paris)*
The northern wall

*...ttack of Snakes. Medallion of the Large Frame.
Panel of the southern wall*
The eastern wall →

as early as November 1941. The inventory of the objects kept in the Königsberg Museum has reached us. An entry on the page dated 5 December 1941, listed as No. 200 the "Amber Room from Tsarskoye Selo". On 12 April 1942 the amber panels were put on display in the south wing of the palace complex. Alfred Rohde, Director of the Art Collections of Königsberg, published in connection with the accession of the Amber Room to the museum an article in the magazine *Pantheon*. The photographic material allows one to notice the lack of one of the Florentine mosaics. Later it was established that the mosaic had been stolen even before the dismantling of the Amber Room in the Catherine Palace.

In 1944, the cities of Germany underwent large-scale attacks of English and American bomber forces while the Soviet troops began to invade Eastern

The Large Frame.
Panel of the southern wall
Detail of the sculptural decor of the Large
Frame. Panel of the southern wall
Florentine mosaic: The Senses of Touch
and Smell. *The southern wall* →

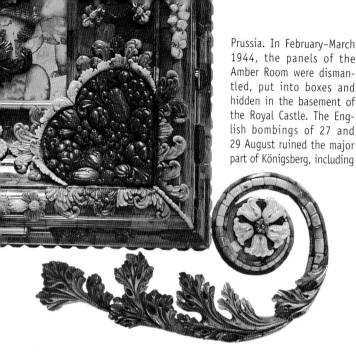

Prussia. In February–March 1944, the panels of the Amber Room were dismantled, put into boxes and hidden in the basement of the Royal Castle. The English bombings of 27 and 29 August ruined the major part of Königsberg, including

the royal complex. However, the decor of the Amber Room, excluding for six lower panels, did not perish. The evacuation of the boxes containing the amber panels from the fighting area began. The further destiny of the Amber Room is unknown, although there are many versions suggesting its present whereabouts.

In the middle of January 1944, as a result of a resolute attack, the Soviet troops liberated Leningrad and its environs. The soldiers who entered the town of Pushkin faced the palaces lying in ruins, with heaps of stones and ashes, charred walls and a complete destruction within the buildings. The once resplendent rooms and halls of the Catherine Palace were devastated and gaped with holes of the broken roofs. Nothing survived from the decor of the Amber Room.

Work on revealing the art values taken away from Soviet museums to Königsberg and the towns of Eastern Prussia started in May 1945. The examination of the Royal Castle in Königsberg yielded the furniture from the Catherine Palace found in one of the towers. Dr. Rohde, who did not left Königsberg, informed that the Amber Room was transferred to the northern part of the building, where it evidently burnt out during the city's assault, between 9 and 11 April 1945. Discovered in the ashes and a layer of stucco were fragments of gilt moulding and copper hinges, presumably from the doors of the Amber Room, as well as the remains of charred planks of boxes. This led to the conclusion that the Amber Room had perished in fire. In March 1946, Alexei Kuchumov, Keeper of the Museum at Tsarskoye Selo, and Stanislav Tronchinsky, Head of the Museum Section in the Department of Culture, the Leningrad Municipal Council, carried out a thorough investigation of all the rooms of the Königsberg Royal Castle.

Detail of the decor of the Large Frame. Panel of the northern wall
Detail of the sculptural decor of the Large Frame. Panel of the southern wall
The lower part of the Large Frame. Panel of the northern wall $\longrightarrow$

Near the outward staircase of the Great Order Room they found thr
charred fragments of the Florentine mosaics. Kuchumov and Tronchi
sky tried to find Rohde. They established that Rohde and his wife di
of dysentery in the municipal hospital in December 1945. There is
opinion that this diagnosis was falsified to disguise the true situati
Systematic research into the problem began in 1967, with the foun
tion of the Commission for Searching the Amber Room. The comm

sion accumulated ample documentation and other information, directly or in some way referring to the Amber Room. The Commission uncovered and explored basements, bunkers, mines and underground depositories. But the great efforts of many people did not yield any positive results. Hopes for a success diminished every year and in December 1984 the activities of the Commission were suspended. It was thought for a long time that the unique cultural monument had perished forever and could not be revived. But there were enthusiasts who made strenuous efforts to explore the secrets of the creation of the "amber miracle". On 10 April 1979 the Council of Ministers took an official

Saul and David. *Medallion of the Large Frame. Panel of the northern wall*
The Healing of Naaman. *Medallion of the Large Frame. Panel of the northern wall*

decision to re-create the Amber Room. The work was entrusted to the Rosmonumentskulptura Company. A model of the panel was produced and the piece was approved as a standard one close to the original. Work on the re-creation of the Amber Room was entrusted to the Leningrad Scientific and Research Amalgamation Restavrator.

During the same years restoration work was under way in the rooms of ⸺ Golden Suite of the Catherine Palace. A group of artists led by Yakov ⸺akov adorned the ceiling of the Amber Room with painting *The Wedding* ⸺ *Chronos* created after sketches by an anonymous seventeenth-century

Details of the amber frame

master. A team of experienced parquetry restorers headed by Yevgeny Kudriashov reproduced the parquet floor of valuable kinds of wood, such as mahogany, sandalwood, walnut, maple

Detail of the upper part of the amber frame. Panel of the northern wall

and palissandre. Alexei Kochuyev's team of woodcarvers was entrusted with the re-creation of the carved decor designed by Rastrelli. A team of gilders under the supervision

Mask and garland in the upper part of the panel

of Natalia Fomicheva overlaid the carved decor with leaf gold. The overall project was worked out by a group of architects under the direction of Alexander Kedrinsky, chief architect responsible for the restoration of the Catherine Palace. To fulfil the task successfully, it was necessary to thoroughly explore the relevant archival, historical and visual materials. The work was based on the photographs preserved in the museum collections of Leningrad. The earliest of them, executed in 1859, belonged to the hand of Théophile Gautier and the last ones, mentioned above as published in the *Pantheon* magazine, were made in 1942. The adjustment of the discovered black-and-white photographs to a single scale enabled the experts to specify the exact dimensions of the

Monogram of Catherine I and decorative frame of a mosaic picture in the Large Frame. Panel of the northern wall

Medallions of the Large Frame. Panel of the northern wall

Detail of the sculptural decor of the Large Frame. Panel of the southern wall

amber panels. During the creation of a detailed drawing of the entire composition tracings from old photographs faithfully reproducing the elements of the background mosaics and the whole three-dimensional decor of each panel in life size were made. A conclusion was also taken to tint amber for attaining various necessary shades. Moreover, life-size sample pieces representing non-repeated individual elements of the wall decor in colour were added to the project.

Eventually Alexander Kedrinsky evolved a detailed re-creation project that comprised six volumes of drawings and documentation referring to its architectural and decorative scheme of the Amber Room. The project was approved in July 1986. It was estimated that the whole amount of work will demand six tons of raw amber — it was established experimentally that due to the specific technology of amber treatment only 15 to 20 percent of the material could be used. Amber necessary to the restorers of the unique interior was supplied for two decades by the Kaliningrad Amber Factory — the only organization in Russia engaged in the excavation of this material.

The shadow cast by a detail on its photograph (method of photogrammetry), allowed the restorers to calculate the height of an amber relief with ultimate precision. The technology of re-creation was developed in the process of restoration of 18th-century amber objec

Mask and garland of the amber overdoor decoration
Detail of the upper part of the Large Frame. The northern wall

48

from the museum's collection undertaken simultaneously with the project. Watercolours by G. Grekhnev produced in the 1850s and kept in the stocks of the museum yielded some additional details about the chromatic decor. The black-and-white photographs made before the war were used to establish a correspondence between the intensity of shades and natural amber. Work with the above-mentioned group of amber articles was also helpful for the establishment of the col-

our scheme of the material used in the eighteenth century. The pigments used then for tinting amber and the methods of colouring were evolved with the assistance of A. Iltsov, Doctor of Chemistry, who was a member of the Council for the Re-creation of the Amber Room.

The re-creation of the Florentine mosaics, an indispensable part of the amber interior, was a long and labour-consuming

*Carved female busts completing
mirror pilasters*

51

process, too. Their specific feature was that the inlays were made of fragments of natural stones remarkable for a variety of textures and shades. The exploration of the mosaic panel *Port at Livorno,* that was executed simultaneously with the mosaics of the Amber Room, helped the restorers to study the technology of their production. So they learned how to replace the lost pieces by the chromatically suitable kinds of stone available in Russia. Information about the deposits of the required minerals was supplied by specialists from the St Petersburg Mining University. Happily, the workshop in Florence, where the mosaics for the Amber Room were produced, exists to this day. It kindly provided information about the technology of stone mosaics. The workshop's

museum has even pre-served colour cartoons of "Allegories of the Five Senses" made for the Amber Room. The Italian colleagues handed over their colour transparencies to Russian master craftsmen.

It took a long time to work out sketches for the panels. This work was made by a creative group including its leader Alexander Kedrinsky, the head of stonecutting work Alexander Zhuravlev, the stonecutters Vladimir Kozlov and Boris Igdalov (later Director of the Tsarskoye Selo Amber Workshop). After studying the techniques of mosaic production, Igdalov recreated the composition *The Sense of Sight*. He was the first in Russia to master the art of reproducing in stone many-figured compositions.

The north-western corner with carved wooden lamps and putti

Nowadays, the process of the re-creation of the amber panels ha
been completed. The basis of the interior design is made up of sculp
tural decoration, profiled framing and micro-relief panel surface
Plaques of opaque amber five millimetres thick were used, which we

The north-western part of the Amber Room
Ceiling painting: The Marriage of Chronos. *After sketches by an anonymous painter of the 17th centur*
Mirror pilasters →

polished and tightly linked one to an other. For three-dimensional compo sitions thoroughly chosen collectibl amber was employed. Present-da craftsmen participating in the repr duction of the amber panels have ma tered this technique to perfection.

Casket. 1705. Danzig, master craftsman G. Turau.
Table commode. First half of the 18th century. Dan
Case for chess and tric-trac.
Early 18th century. Danzig
Powder-case. First half of the 18th century.
North Germany
Box. Late 17th – early 18th century.
Danzig

On 31 May 2003, the jubilee of St Petersburg, the ceremony of the inauguration of the Amber Room was held. The unique interior with its fine decor celebrating the beauty of the "sunny stone", has become the culminating accomplishment of the stonecutter's art of the past and present. One of the greatest wonders that caused admiration throughout two centuries has been recreated by the efforts of our contemporaries and will delight generations to come.

Pineapple-shaped soap-box from the Cavaliers' set
Cavalier's set. 1764
The Tsarskoye Selo Amber Workshop
Little samovar with a tray and pipe.
Late 18th century (?).
St Petersburg
The southern wall →

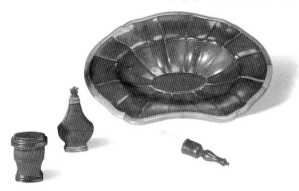

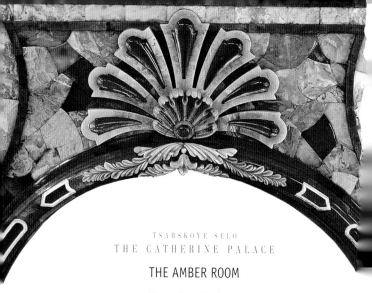

TSARSKOYE SELO
THE CATHERINE PALACE

THE AMBER ROOM

Text by Victoria Plaude
Translated from the Russian by Valery Fateyev
Designed by Piotr Kanaikin
Photographs by Valentin Baranovsky, Sergei Chistobayev,
Vladimir Davydov, Pavel Demidov, Vladimir Denisov, Alexander Kashnitsky,
Victor Savik, Yevgeny Siniaver and Oleg Trubsky, Vasily Vorontsov

ISBN 5-93893-205-X